THE WORLD OF FUDGE

116 DELICIOUS AND QUICK FUDGE RECIPES TO ENJOY WITH FAMILY AND FRIENDS.
SUITABLE FOR BEGINNERS.

BY LIAM TORRES

Table Of Contents

Table Of Contents

Table Of Contents

Table Of Contents

Fudge Crackles

Ingredients

7 (1 ounce) squares semisweet chocolate
2 (1 ounce) squares unsweetened chocolate
3 tablespoons butter, softened
1 cup white sugar
3 eggs
1 teaspoon vanilla extract
3/4 cup all-purpose flour
1/2 teaspoon baking powder
1/4 teaspoon salt
1 cup semisweet chocolate chips
1/2 cup chopped walnuts

Directions

Chop chocolate and melt with 3 tablespoons butter or margarine in the top of a double boiler over simmering water. Stir until melted. Remove from hot water and cool slightly.

Mix together flour, baking powder and salt and set aside.

Beat together sugar and eggs until thick and creamy. Mix in vanilla and melted chocolate. Add flour mixture until well blended. Add chocolate chips and nuts.

Drop by teaspoonfuls about 1-1/2 inches apart on greased cookie sheet. Bake in a 350 degrees F (175 degrees C) oven for 8 minutes or until tops are cracked and shiny. Cool on sheet 3-5 minutes. Remove to racks to cool completely.

Made-in-Minutes No-Cook Fudge

Ingredients

1 cup virgin coconut oil, room temperature
1 cup unsweetened cocoa powder
1/2 cup honey

Directions

Lightly grease 8x8 inch baking dish.

Pour the coconut oil into a bowl, and sift in the cocoa, stirring to blend evenly. Stir in the honey, and mix until smooth. Spread mixture into prepared dish, and refrigerate at least 1 hour. Cut into 1 inch squares.

Fudge

Ingredients

3 cups semisweet chocolate chips
1 (14 ounce) can sweetened condensed milk
1/4 cup butter
1 cup chopped walnuts (optional)

Directions

Place chocolate chips, sweetened condensed milk, and butter or margarine in large microwaveable bowl. Zap in microwave on medium until chips are melted, about 3-5 minute, stirring once or twice during cooking. Stir in nuts, if desired.

Pour into well-greased 8x8-inch glass baking dish. Refrigerate until set.

Peanut Butter Fudge II

Ingredients

2 cups peanut butter chips
1 cup semisweet chocolate chips
1/2 cup butter
1 (14 ounce) can sweetened
condensed milk

Directions

Line a 9x9 inch square pan with wax paper.

In a medium sized saucepan, melt butter over medium heat. Stir in the condensed milk. Add the peanut butter and chocolate chips, stirring constantly until everything is melted and blended together.

Pour the mixture into the prepared pan and refrigerate for 3 hours. Cut into squares when cool. Comes out perfect every time!

Marshmallow Fudge Bars

Ingredients

2 cups white sugar
1/4 cup unsweetened cocoa powder
1 cup butter, melted
4 eggs
2 teaspoons vanilla extract
1 1/2 cups all-purpose flour
3/4 teaspoon baking powder
1 teaspoon salt
1/2 cup chopped walnuts

1 (16 ounce) package miniature marshmallows

1/2 cup brown sugar
1/4 cup water
1 (1 ounce) square unsweetened baking chocolate
1 tablespoon butter
1 teaspoon vanilla extract
1 1/2 cups confectioners' sugar

Directions

Preheat oven to 350 degrees F (175 degrees C). Grease a 9x13 inch baking pan.

In a large bowl, stir together the white sugar and cocoa. Mix in the melted butter until well blended. Beat in the eggs one at a time, then stir in 2 teaspoons vanilla. Combine the flour, baking powder and salt; stir into the chocolate mixture. Fold in walnuts. Spread evenly into the prepared pan.

Bake for 30 minutes in the preheated oven, until the cake starts to pull away from the sides of the pan. Remove from the oven and cover with an even layer of miniature marshmallows. Return to the oven for about 2 to 3 minutes longer. Remove from the oven and allow to cool in the pan.

In a small saucepan over medium heat, combine brown sugar, water and unsweetened chocolate. Bring to a boil and boil for 3 minutes. Stir in 1 tablespoon butter and 1 teaspoon vanilla until well blended. Mix in the confectioners' sugar until smooth. Spread over the marshmallow layer. Allow frosting to set before cutting into bars.

Tofu Fudge Mocha Bars

Ingredients

1 (12 ounce) package silken tofu, undrained
2 tablespoons safflower oil
1 pinch salt
2 1/3 cups turbinado sugar
1 cup cocoa powder
1/3 cup instant decaffeinated coffee powder
1 teaspoon vanilla extract
1 cup whole wheat flour

Directions

Preheat oven to 325 degrees F (165 degrees C).

Using an electric mixer, blend tofu until creamy. Add oil, salt, sugar, cocoa, coffee and vanilla and blend well.

When sugar is dissolved into the tofu mixture remove the bowl from the electric mixer and whisk in flour.

Pour batter into a greased 9x13 inch baking pan.

Bake 25 to 30 minutes, or until the cake pulls away from the side of the pan. The bars will appear glossy, almost underdone. Cool in the pan and when cool cut into bars using a clean, wet knife.

White Christmas Fudge

Ingredients

3 cups white sugar, divided
2 tablespoons water, divided
2 egg whites
1 cup corn syrup
1 1/2 teaspoons vanilla extract
1 cup pecans

Directions

In a medium saucepan over medium heat combine 1 cup sugar with 1 tablespoon water. Heat to between 234 and 240 degrees F (112 to 116 degrees C), or until a small amount of syrup dropped into cold water forms a soft ball that flattens when removed from the water and placed on a flat surface. Stir in egg whites and vanilla.

In a separate saucepan combine remaining 2 cups sugar, corn syrup and 1 tablespoon water; heat to 250 to 265 degrees F (121 to 129 degrees C), or until a small amount of syrup dropped into cold water forms a rigid ball. Stir this mixture into the other pan with sugar.

To the sugar mixture add nuts. Pour into a 9 x 9 inch dish and chill until firm. Cut into 1 inch squares.

Grandpa's Peanut Butter Fudge

Ingredients

2 cups brown sugar
2 cups white sugar
1 cup milk
1 1/2 cups creamy peanut butter
1 tablespoon margarine
1 1/4 teaspoons vanilla extract

Directions

Mix brown and white sugar with the milk in large pot; bring mixture to a boil. Stir in peanut butter, reduce heat to medium and bring the mixture back to boil (stirring constantly). Remove the pot from heat when a drop of the mixture forms a ball in a glass of cold water.

Stir margarine and vanilla into the mixture; stir vigorously until the fudge hardens. (Always stir in same direction.) Pour fudge onto buttered plates or waxed paper. Let cool and cut into 1 inch pieces.

Mocha Fudge

Ingredients

1 tablespoon instant coffee granules
3 cups white sugar
1 pinch salt
1 cup milk
2 tablespoons light corn syrup
3 tablespoons butter
1 teaspoon vanilla extract
1/2 cup chopped pecans
1 cup semisweet chocolate chips
1/2 cup pecan halves, for decoration (optional)

Directions

In a medium saucepan, stir together the instant coffee, white sugar and salt. Stir in the milk and corn syrup, and add the butter. Heat to between 234 and 240 degrees F (112 to 116 degrees C), or until a small amount of syrup dropped into cold water forms a soft ball that flattens when removed from the water and placed on a flat surface. Remove from heat, and stir in vanilla. Let cool to room temperature, or about 110 degrees F (45 degrees C).

When the mixture is cool, beat with a wooden spoon until it loses its gloss. Add nuts and chocolate chips and stir slightly to create a marbled effect. Pour into a buttered 8 inch square baking dish. Arrange pecan halves on the top if desired. Cool completely before cutting into pieces.

Best Ever Chocolate Fudge Layer Cake

Ingredients

1 (18.25 ounce) package chocolate cake mix
1 pkg. (4 serving size) JELL-O Chocolate Flavor Instant Pudding & Pie Filling
4 eggs
1 cup BREAKSTONE'S or KNUDSEN Sour Cream
1/2 cup oil
1/2 cup water
1 (8 ounce) package BAKER'S Semi-Sweet Baking Chocolate, divided
1 (8 ounce) tub COOL WHIP Whipped Topping, thawed
2 tablespoons PLANTERS Sliced Almonds

Directions

Preheat oven to 350 degrees F. Lightly grease 2 (9-inch) round cake pans. Beat cake mix, dry pudding mix, eggs, sour cream, oil and water in large bowl with electric mixer on low speed just until moistened, scraping side of bowl frequently. Beat on medium speed 2 min. or until well blended. Stir in 2 squares of the chocolate, chopped. Spoon into prepared pans.

Bake 30 to 35 min. or until toothpick inserted near centers comes out clean. Cool in pans 10 min. on wire rack. Loosen cakes from side of pans with spatula or knife. Invert cakes onto rack; gently remove pans. Cool completely on wire rack.

Place remaining 6 squares chocolate and whipped topping in medium microwaveable bowl. Microwave on HIGH 1-1/2 to 2 min. Stir until well blended and shiny. Cool 5 min. Place 1 cake layer on serving plate; spread 1/4 of the chocolate mixture over cake. Place second cake layer on top; spread remaining chocolate mixture over top and sides of cake. Garnish with almonds.

Peanut Butter Fudge III

Ingredients

1 (12 fluid ounce) can evaporated milk
1/2 cup butter
5 cups white sugar
1 pinch salt
1 (16 ounce) jar peanut butter
1 (7 ounce) jar marshmallow creme
1 teaspoon vanilla extract

Directions

Grease a 9x13 inch pan.

In a large saucepan with a candy thermometer inserted, pour evaporated milk, butter or margarine, sugar, and salt. Bring to a boil and cook until candy thermometer reads 236 degrees F (115 degrees C). Remove from heat.

Stir in peanut butter, marshmallow creme, and vanilla extract Mix well and pour immediately into prepared pan. Allow to cool completely, then cut into pieces.

Butterscotch Peanut Fudge

Ingredients

1 (14 ounce) can sweetened condensed milk
1 (11 ounce) package butterscotch chips
1 1/2 cups miniature marshmallows
2/3 cup peanut butter
1 teaspoon vanilla extract
1 cup chopped salted peanuts

Directions

In a microwave-safe bowl, combine the milk, butterscotch chips and marshmallows. Microwave, uncovered, at 80% power for 3 minutes or until chips and marshmallows are melted, stirring frequently. Stir in peanut butter and vanilla until combined. Fold in the peanuts.

Pour into an 11-in. x 7-in. x 2-in. pan coated with nonstick cooking spray. Cover and refrigerate for 2 hours or until firm. Cut into squares. Store in the refrigerator.

Wellesley Fudge Cake II

Ingredients

1/2 cup butter
1 7/8 cups white sugar
4 egg yolks
1 cup all-purpose flour
1 cup unsweetened cocoa powder
1 1/3 tablespoons baking powder
1/2 teaspoon salt
4 egg whites
1 cup milk
2 teaspoons vanilla extract

2 cups semisweet chocolate chips
3/4 cup sour cream
1 teaspoon vanilla extract
1 pinch salt

Directions

Preheat oven to 325 degrees F (165 degrees C). Grease and flour three 9 inch round cake pans.

In a large bowl, cream together the butter and sugar. Beat in the egg yolks, one at a time. Stir in 2 teaspoons vanilla. Combine the flour, cocoa, baking powder and salt, stir into the creamed mixture alternately with the milk.

In a large clean glass or metal bowl, whip egg whites until soft peaks form. Fold 1/3 of whites into batter to lighten it, then quickly fold in remaining whites until no streaks remain. Divide batter into the 3 prepared pans.

Bake for 20 to 25 minutes in the preheated oven, until a toothpick inserted into the center of the cake comes out clean. Cool in pans on a wire rack.

To make the frosting: Melt the chocolate chips in the top of a double boiler, stirring occasionally until smooth. Remove from heat and stir in the sour cream, 1 teaspoon vanilla and pinch of salt. Frosting can be used warm to fill and frost the 3 layers.

Creamy Orange Fudge

Ingredients

2 pounds white chocolate, melted
2 (8 ounce) packages cream cheese
6 cups confectioners' sugar
1 tablespoon orange extract

Directions

Beat cream cheese into melted chocolate until well blended. Beat in confectioner's sugar until mixture is smooth. Stir in orange extract. Spread in an 8x8 inch dish and let set before cutting into squares. Store in refrigerator.

Chocolate Fudge Cupcakes with Peanut Butter

Ingredients

Cupcakes
1 (19.5 ounce) package
PillsburyB® Brownie Classics
Traditional Fudge Brownie Mix
2 eggs
1/2 cup CriscoB® All-Vegetable
Oil
1/4 cup water
1 1/2 cups semi-sweet chocolate
chips

Frosting
1 (12 ounce) container
PillsburyB® Vanilla FunfettiB®
Frosting
3/4 cup JifB® Creamy Peanut
Butter

Directions

Heat oven to 350 degrees F. Position a rack in the middle of the oven. Line 18 regular muffin cups with paper cupcake liners.

Mix brownie mix, eggs, oil and water in a medium mixing bowl until well blended. Fill the muffin cups half full with brownie batter. Place about 1 tablespoon chocolate chips in the center of the batter.

Bake 18-20 minutes or until set. Cool slightly. Remove from muffin pans and let cool completely on wire racks.

Stir together frosting and peanut butter in a medium bowl. Spread over top of cooled cupcakes. Using the container of sprinkles included with the frosting, decorate the top of each cupcake.

Vegan Peanut Butter Fudge

Ingredients

2 cups packed brown sugar
1/8 teaspoon salt
3/4 cup soy milk
2 tablespoons light corn syrup
4 tablespoons peanut butter
1 teaspoon vanilla extract

Directions

Lightly grease one 9x5x2 inch pan.

In a 2-quart pot over very low heat, mix together the brown sugar, salt, soy milk, corn syrup, peanut butter and vanilla. Cook until hot and brown sugar is dissolved.

Quickly pour into pan and refrigerate. Cut into squares and store in semi-airtight container in refrigerator.

Chocolate Fudge

Ingredients

3 cups white sugar
1 cup evaporated milk
1/4 cup unsweetened cocoa
powder
1/4 cup creamy peanut butter

Directions

In a 3 quart saucepan, combine white sugar, evaporated milk, and cocoa. Bring to a hard boil, and then reduce heat to medium. Continue cooking until it reaches the soft ball stage, 234 degrees F (112 degrees C).

Stir in peanut butter until well blended. Pour mixture into a buttered 8x8 inch baking dish. Cool, and cut into pieces.

Fabulous Fudge Chocolate Cake

Ingredients

2 1/4 cups all-purpose flour
2 teaspoons baking soda
1/2 teaspoon salt
1/2 cup butter
2 1/2 cups packed brown sugar
3 eggs
1 1/2 teaspoons vanilla extract
3 (1 ounce) squares unsweetened chocolate, melted
1 cup sour cream
1 cup boiling water
1/2 cup butter
1 cup packed brown sugar
1/4 cup milk
1 3/4 cups confectioners' sugar

Directions

Preheat oven to 350 degrees F (175 degrees C).

Sift together the flour, baking soda and salt. Set aside.

In a large bowl, beat 1/2 cup butter or margarine and 2 1/2 cups brown sugar until well mixed. Add eggs one at a time. Beat in the vanilla and melted chocolate squares. Add 1/2 the sour cream and then 1/2 the dry ingredients to the butter mixture until well blended.

Add the remaining sour cream and dry ingredients to the batter. Stir in boiling water.

Bake in a greased 9 X 13 inch pan for 35 minutes.

Let cool 10 minutes before icing.

To Make Caramel Icing: First melt 1/2 cup butter in a saucepan. Stir in 1 cup brown sugar and boil about 2 minutes. Stir in 1/4 cup milk and bring to a boil. Place pan in cold water and stir in the confectioners' sugar. Continue stirring until smooth. Spread over still warm cake.

Banana Fudge Cake

Ingredients

1 (18.25 ounce) package chocolate fudge cake mix
1 large ripe banana, mashed
FROSTING:
1/2 cup butter or margarine
1/4 cup water
5 1/2 cups confectioners' sugar, divided
1/4 cup baking cocoa
1 small ripe banana, mashed
1/2 teaspoon vanilla extract

Directions

In a mixing bowl, prepare cake mix according to package directions, omitting 1/4 cup of the water. Beat on low speed until moistened. Add banana; beat on high for 2 minutes. Pour into a greased 13-in. x 9-in. x 2-in. baking pan. Bake at 350 degrees F for 35-40 minutes or until a toothpick inserted near the center comes out clean. Cool completely. In a saucepan, heat butter and water until butter is melted; set aside. In a mixing bowl, combine 4 cups confectioners' sugar and cocoa. Add butter mixture, banana and vanilla; beat until smooth. Add enough remaining sugar until frosting reaches desired spreading consistency. Frost the cake.

Maple Fudge

Ingredients

2 cups maple syrup
1 tablespoon light corn syrup
3/4 cup light cream
1 teaspoon vanilla extract
3/4 cup chopped walnuts

Directions

Butter an 8x8 inch dish.

In a medium saucepan, combine maple syrup, corn syrup, and cream. Bring to a boil, stirring constantly. Then heat without stirring to between 234 and 240 degrees F (112 to 116 degrees C), or until a small amount of syrup dropped into cold water forms a soft ball that flattens when removed from the water and placed on a flat surface. Remove from heat, and let cool until lukewarm.

Beat mixture until it thickens and loses its gloss. Quickly fold in vanilla and nuts, and spread in prepared pan. Let cool completely before cutting.

Hot Fudge Frosting

Ingredients

3 (1 ounce) squares unsweetened chocolate
2 tablespoons butter 1/2
cup light corn syrup 1/2
cup white sugar
1/4 cup milk
1 teaspoon vanilla extract

Directions

In a saucepan on very low heat, carefully melt the chocolate and butter, stirring constantly. Add the corn syrup, sugar, and milk. Increase heat to medium-high, bring to a boil, and cook for 5-8 minutes, stirring only occasionally, until the mixture becomes a candy-like, gooey fudge. Remove from heat and stir in vanilla. Let chill to spreadable consistency.

Brazilian Peanut Fudge

Ingredients

1 (8 ounce) jar roasted peanuts, skins removed
1 (8 ounce) package tea biscuits (such as Marie Biscuits)
2 tablespoons white sugar
1 (14 ounce) can sweetened condensed milk

Directions

Line a 9-inch square dish with waxed paper.

Pulse the peanuts and biscuits together in a food processor until the mixture resembles coarse flour. Add the sugar and pulse to mix. Pour the sweetened, condensed milk into the mixture and process until the mixture forms a ball that pulls away from the sides of the food processor bowl.

Transfer the mixture to the prepared dish and press with your hands into an even layer. Allow to sit at least 15 minutes, up to overnight. Remove from the dish and cut into squares to serve. Store in airtight containers between uses.

Ingredients

4 (1 ounce) squares unsweetened chocolate
1 cup white sugar
1/8 teaspoon salt
1 tablespoon butter
1 cup heavy cream
1/2 teaspoon vanilla extract

Directions

Place chocolate in a microwave safe bowl and cook on high 1 to 2 minutes, stirring frequently, until mostly melted. Transfer to a heavy-bottomed saucepan over low heat and stir in sugar, salt and butter. Stir in cream, a little at a time until smooth. Heat through, without boiling, then remove from heat and stir in vanilla. Store in refrigerator.

Fudge Bonbons

Ingredients

2 cups semisweet chocolate chips
1/4 cup butter
1 (14 ounce) can sweetened condensed milk
2 cups all-purpose flour
1 teaspoon vanilla extract
60 milk chocolate candy kisses, unwrapped

Directions

Preheat oven to 350 degrees F (175 degrees C). In a heavy saucepan over low heat, stir chocolate chips and butter until melted and smooth. Stir in condensed milk, flour and vanilla until well blended.

Shape one level teaspoon of chocolate chip dough around each candy kiss. Arrange bonbons one inch apart on ungreased cookie sheets.

Bake 6 minutes. Bonbons will be soft and shiny, but will firm up as they cool.

Pumpkin Fudge

Ingredients

2 tablespoons butter
2 1/2 cups white sugar
2/3 cup evaporated milk
1 cup white chocolate chips
7 ounces marshmallow creme
3/4 cup canned pumpkin
1 teaspoon ground cinnamon
1 teaspoon vanilla extract

Directions

Line a 9x9 inch pan with aluminum foil, and set aside.

In a 3 quart saucepan, heat milk and sugar over medium heat. Bring to a boil, stirring occasionally with a wooden spoon.

Mix in pumpkin puree and cinnamon; bring back to a boil. Stir in marshmallow creme and butter. Bring to a rolling boil. Cook, stirring occasionally, for 18 minutes.

Remove from heat, and add white chocolate chips and vanilla. Stir until creamy and all chips are melted. Pour into prepared pan. Cool, remove from pan, and cut into squares. Store in a cool, dry place.

Velvety Walnut Fudge Pie

Ingredients

1 (3.5 ounce) package non-instant chocolate fudge pudding mix
3/4 cup light corn syrup
1 egg
1 cup chopped walnuts
3/4 cup evaporated milk
1/2 cup semisweet chocolate chips
1 recipe pastry for a 9 inch single crust pie

Directions

Melt the chocolate chips.

In a large bowl, combine pie filling, evaporated milk, corn syrup, egg, melted chocolate chips. Stir in nuts. Pour into pie shell.

Bake at 375 degrees F (175 degrees C) for about 45 minutes; bake until top is firm and begins to crack. Cool at least 4 hours. Garnish with whipped cream if desired.

Baked Fudge Cake

Ingredients

4 eggs
2 cups white sugar
1/2 cup all-purpose flour 1/2
cup unsweetened cocoa 1/2
teaspoon salt
1 cup butter, melted
2 teaspoons vanilla extract
1 cup chopped pecans

Directions

Preheat oven to 325 degrees F (165 degrees C). Grease and flour an 8x8 inch pan. In a food processor or blender, beat eggs for 2 minutes.

In a large bowl, mix together the sugar, flour, cocoa and salt. Slowly beat in the whipped eggs. Beat in the butter and vanilla. Stir in the chopped pecans. Spread batter in prepared pan.

Bake in the preheated oven for 45 to 50 minutes, or until a toothpick inserted into the center of the cake comes out clean. Allow to cool.

Brownies with Peanut Butter Fudge Frosting

Ingredients

1 (19.8 ounce) package brownie mix
1 cup peanut butter chips
1/2 cup butter
1 (14 ounce) can sweetened condensed milk

Directions

Bake brownies according to package directions. Allow them to cool in the pan. Do not cut.

In a medium saucepan over low heat, melt peanut butter chips and butter together, stirring frequently until smooth. Remove from heat and stir in the sweetened condensed milk. Spread evenly over the cooled brownies. Chill until set and cut into squares.

Raspberry Fudge Balls

Ingredients

1 cup semisweet chocolate chips
1 (8 ounce) package cream cheese, softened
3/4 cup vanilla wafer crumbs
1/4 cup seedless raspberry jam
3/4 cup finely chopped almonds

Directions

In a microwave or heavy saucepan, melt chocolate chips; stir until smooth. Cool slightly. In a mixing bowl, beat the cream cheese and melted chocolate until smooth. Stir in the wafer crumbs and jam. Refrigerate for 4 hours or until firm. Shape into 1-in. balls; roll in almonds. Store in an airtight container in the refrigerator.

Joan's Fudge Icing

Ingredients

4 cups white sugar
1 cup shortening
1 cup heavy whipping cream
1/2 cup corn syrup
1 teaspoon salt
2 (1 ounce) squares semisweet chocolate, grated
2 teaspoons vanilla extract

Directions

Combine sugar, shortening, cream, corn syrup, salt and slivered chocolate in a saucepan. Cook over low heat until chocolate and shortening melt, stirring continuously. Bring to rolling boil 220 degrees F (105 degrees C) and hold one minute. Remove from heat and begin beating and beat until 120 degrees F (49 degrees C). Add vanilla and beat to spreading consistency.

Best-Ever Chocolate Fudge Layer Cake

Ingredients

1 (8 ounce) package BAKER'S Semi-Sweet Baking Chocolate, divided
1 (18.25 ounce) package chocolate cake mix
1 pkg. (4 serving size) JELL-O Chocolate Flavor Instant Pudding & Pie Filling
4 eggs
1 cup BREAKSTONE'S or KNUDSEN Sour Cream
1/2 cup oil
1/2 cup water
1 (8 ounce) tub COOL WHIP Whipped Topping, thawed
2 tablespoons PLANTERS Sliced Almonds

Directions

Preheat oven to 350 degrees F. Grease two 9-inch round baking pans. Chop 2 of the chocolate squares; set aside. Beat cake mix, dry pudding mix, eggs, sour cream, oil and water in large bowl with electric mixer on low speed just until moistened. Beat on medium speed 2 min. Stir in chopped chocolate. Spoon into prepared pans.

Bake 30 to 35 min. or until wooden toothpick inserted in centers comes out clean. Cool in pans on wire racks 10 min. Loosen cakes from sides of pans. Invert onto racks; gently remove pans. Cool cakes completely.

Place frozen whipped topping and remaining 6 chocolate squares in microwaveable bowl. Microwave on HIGH 1-1/2 min. or until chocolate is completely melted and mixture is smooth, stirring after 1 min. Let stand 15 min. to thicken. Place one cake layer on serving plate; top with one-fourth of the chocolate mixture and second cake layer. Spread top and side with remaining chocolate mixture. Garnish with almonds. Store leftovers in refrigerator.

Million Dollar Fudge

Ingredients

4 1/2 cups white sugar
1 pinch salt
2 tablespoons butter
1 (12 fluid ounce) can evaporated milk
2 cups chopped nuts
1 (12 ounce) package semisweet chocolate chips
12 (1 ounce) squares German sweet chocolate
2 cups marshmallow creme

Directions

Butter two 9x9 inch baking pans and set aside.

Place chocolate chips, German chocolate, marshmallow creme, and nuts into a large mixing bowl. Set aside.

In a 4 quart saucepan, combine sugar, salt, butter, and evaporated milk. Stir over low heat until the sugar dissolves. Bring to a boil, and cook for 6 minutes.

Pour boiling syrup over ingredients in bowl, beat until all chocolate is melted. Pour into prepared pans. Let stand a few hours before cutting.

Tunnel of Fudge Cake IV

Ingredients

3/4 cups margarine, softened
3/4 cups white sugar
eggs
2 cups confectioners' sugar
2 1/4 cups all-purpose flour
3/4 cup unsweetened cocoa
powder
cups chopped walnuts

3/4 cup confectioners' sugar
1/4 cup unsweetened cocoa
powder
2 tablespoons milk

Directions

Preheat oven to 350 degrees F (175 degrees C). Grease and flour a 10 inch Bundt pan.

In a large bowl, cream together the butter and white sugar until light and fluffy. Beat in the eggs one at a time. Gradually blend in 2 cups confectioners' sugar. Beat in the flour and 3/4 cup cocoa powder. Stir in the chopped walnuts. Pour batter into prepared pan.

Bake in the preheated oven for 60 to 65 minutes, or until a toothpick inserted into the center of the cake comes out clean. Let cool in pan for 1 hour, then turn out onto a wire rack and cool completely.

For the glaze: In a small bowl, combine 3/4 cup confectioners' sugar and 1/4 cup cocoa. Stir in milk, a tablespoon at a time, until desired drizzling consistency is achieved. Spoon over cake.

White Chocolate Fudge Cake

Ingredients

1 (18.25 ounce) package white cake mix
1 1/4 cups water
3 egg whites
1/3 cup vegetable oil
1 teaspoon vanilla extract
3 (1 ounce) squares white chocolate, melted
FILLING:
3/4 cup semisweet chocolate chips
2 tablespoons butter (no substitutes)
FROSTING:
1 (16 ounce) can vanilla frosting
3 (1 ounce) squares white chocolate, melted
1 teaspoon vanilla extract
1 (8 ounce) carton frozen whipped topping, thawed

Directions

In a mixing bowl, combine the dry cake mix, water, egg whites, oil and vanilla. Beat on low for 2 minutes. Stir in white chocolate. Pour into a greased 13-in. x 9-in. x 2-in. baking pan. Bake at 350 degrees F for 25-30 minutes or until a toothpick inserted near the center comes out clean. Cool for 5 minutes.

Meanwhile, in a microwave or heavy saucepan over low heat, melt chocolate chips and butter; stir until smooth. Carefully spread over warm cake. Cool completely.

In a mixing bowl, beat frosting; stir in white chocolate and vanilla. Fold in whipped topping; frost cake. Store in the refrigerator.

Sue's Hot Fudge Sauce

Ingredients

cup butter

/3 cup unsweetened cocoa
powder

cups white sugar

(12 fluid ounce) can evaporated
milk

teaspoon vanilla extract

Directions

Combine butter, cocoa, sugar and evaporated milk in a saucepan over medium heat. Bring to a boil and boil for 7 minutes. Remove from heat; stir in vanilla. Carefully pour hot mixture into a blender and blend for 2 to 4 minutes. Serve immediately. Store in refrigerator.

Microwavable Chocolate Fudge

Ingredients

2 cups semisweet chocolate chips
1 (14 ounce) can sweetened condensed milk
2 teaspoons vanilla extract
1 1/2 cups chopped walnuts (optional)
1 cup miniature marshmallows

Directions

Grease an 8x8 inch square pan.

Place the chocolate chips and sweetened condensed milk into a medium sized microwavable bowl. Microwave on high for 2 to 3 minutes, stirring occasionally, until smooth. Stir in the vanilla, then fold in the walnuts and marshmallows. Spread evenly into the prepared pan. Chill until set.

Hot Fudge Pudding Cake III

Ingredients

1 cup all-purpose flour
2 teaspoons baking powder
1/4 teaspoon salt
3/4 cup white sugar
2 tablespoons unsweetened cocoa powder
1/2 cup milk
2 tablespoons butter, melted
1 cup brown sugar
1/4 cup unsweetened cocoa powder
1 3/4 cups hot water

Directions

Preheat oven to 350 degrees F (175 degrees C). Grease and flour a 9 inch square pan.

In a medium bowl, mix together the flour, baking powder, salt, sugar, and cocoa. Stir in the milk and melted butter. Spread evenly into the prepared pan.

In a small bowl, combine the brown sugar and cocoa. Spread over the top of the batter in the pan. Pour the hot water over the entire pan of batter.

Bake for 45 minutes in the preheated oven. The cake is done when the cake part is on top and the bottom is of a pudding consistency.

Old Fashioned Fudge Cookies

Ingredients

1 cup white sugar
3/4 cup butter, softened
1 egg
2 teaspoons vanilla extract
2 1/4 cups all-purpose flour
1 teaspoon baking powder
1/4 teaspoon salt
4 (1 ounce) squares unsweetened chocolate, melted

Directions

Cream sugar and butter in mixer till creamy. Add eggs and vanilla, beat till well-mixed.

Blend in flour, baking powder, and salt. Continue beating until well mixed. Beat in melted chocolate on low speed just until mixed.

Shape into slightly flattened balls (rounded teaspoonfuls). Bake on ungreased cookie sheets at 375 degrees F (190 degrees C) for 7-8 minutes or until set. Cool for about a minute, then remove to wire racks to cool.

Envelopes of Fudge

Ingredients

1/2 cup butter (no substitutes), softened

1 (3 ounce) package cream cheese, softened

1 1/4 cups all-purpose flour

FILLING:

1/2 cup sugar

1/3 cup baking cocoa

1/4 cup butter (no substitutes), softened

1 egg yolk

1/2 teaspoon vanilla extract

1/8 teaspoon salt

1/2 cup finely chopped walnuts

Directions

In a mixing bowl, cream butter and cream cheese. Gradually add the flour. On a lightly floured surface, knead until smooth, about 3 minutes. Cover and refrigerate for 1-2 hours or until easy to handle. For filling, combine the sugar, cocoa, butter, yolk, vanilla and salt. Stir in walnuts; set aside. On a lightly floured surface, roll into a 12 -1/2-in. square; cut into 2-1/2-in. squares. Place a rounded teaspoonful of filling in center of each square. Bring two opposite corners to center. Moisten edges with water and pinch together. Place 1 in. apart on lightly greased baking sheets. Bake at 350 degrees F for 18-22 minutes or until lightly browned. Remove to wire racks to cool.

Old Fashioned Fudge Cake

Ingredients

1 cup water
1 cup unsalted butter
4 (1 ounce) squares unsweetened chocolate, chopped
2 cups all-purpose flour
2 cups white sugar
1/2 teaspoon baking soda
1/2 cup sour cream
2 eggs
1 teaspoon vanilla extract

Directions

Preheat oven to 350 degrees F (175 degrees C). Grease and flour a 9 inch tube pan. In small saucepan, heat butter, chocolate and water until chocolate melts and mixture is smooth, stirring constantly. Set aside to cool.

Sift together into a large bowl the flour, sugar and baking soda. In a small bowl, beat egg slightly and combine with sour cream and vanilla. Stir into flour mixture. Pour in the cooled chocolate mixture. Beat at low speed for 5 minutes until completely combined and the consistency of heavy cream.

Pour batter into prepared 9 inch tube pan. Bake in the preheated oven for 45 to 60 minutes, or until a toothpick inserted into the center of the cake comes out clean. Let cool in pan for 10 minutes, then turn out onto a wire rack and cool completely.

Strawberry Fudge

Ingredients

1 (12 fluid ounce) can evaporated milk
3 cups white sugar
2 tablespoons butter
1 3/4 cups sliced fresh strawberries
2 tablespoons lemon juice

Directions

Butter a 9x9 inch dish.

Combine milk, sugar and butter in a large saucepan over medium heat; boil. Stir in strawberries and lemon juice. Heat, stirring constantly, to between 234 and 240 degrees F (112 to 116 degrees C), or until a small amount of syrup dropped into cold water forms a soft ball that flattens when removed from the water and placed on a flat surface.

Remove from heat and quickly spread in prepared pan. Let cool before cutting and serving.

Double Chocolate Fudge

Ingredients

1 (12 ounce) package semisweet chocolate chips
1 (14 ounce) can sweetened condensed milk, divided
2 teaspoons vanilla extract, divided
1 cup chopped walnuts, divided
1 (11.5 ounce) package milk chocolate chips

Directions

Line a 9-in. square pan with foil and butter the foil; set aside. In a heavy saucepan, melt semisweet chocolate chips with 1/2 cup plus 3 tablespoons milk over low heat. Remove from the heat; stir in 1 teaspoon vanilla 1/2 cup walnuts. Spread into prepared pan. In a saucepan, melt milk chocolate chips with remaining milk. Remove from the heat; stir in remaining vanilla and walnuts. Spread over first layer. Cover and refrigerate until firm. Remove from pan and cut into 1-in. squares. Store at room temperature.

Chocolate Walnut Fudge

Ingredients

1/2 cup butter
1 cup semisweet chocolate chips
1 teaspoon vanilla extract
2 cups white sugar
1 (5 ounce) can evaporated milk
10 large marshmallows
1 cup chopped walnuts

Directions

Butter an 8x8 inch dish.

Place butter, chocolate chips and vanilla in a mixing bowl. Set aside.

In a medium saucepan over medium heat, combine sugar, milk and marshmallows. Bring to a boil, stirring frequently. Reduce heat to low and cook 6 minutes more, stirring constantly. Remove from heat.

Pour marshmallow mixture over contents of mixing bowl. Beat entire mixture until it thickens and loses its gloss. Quickly fold in nuts and pour into prepared pan. Refrigerate several hours until firm.

Orange Cream Fudge

Ingredients

3 cups white sugar 2/3
cup heavy cream 3/4
cup butter
1 (7 ounce) jar marshmallow
creme
1 (11 ounce) package white
chocolate chips
3 teaspoons orange extract
12 drops yellow food coloring
9 drops red food coloring

Directions

Grease a 9 x 13 inch pan.

In a medium saucepan over medium heat, combine sugar, cream and butter. Heat to soft ball stage, 234 degrees F (112 degrees C). Remove from heat and stir in marshmallow creme and white chocolate chips; mix well until the chips melt. Reserve 1 cup of mixture and set aside.

To the remaining mixture add orange flavoring, yellow and red food coloring. Stir well and pour into prepared pan. Pour reserved cream mixture on top. Using a knife, swirl layers for decorative effect.

Chill for 2 hours, or until firm, and cut into squares.

Layered Mint Chocolate Fudge

Ingredients

2 cups semi-sweet chocolate chips
1 (14 ounce) can EAGLE BRAND® Sweetened Condensed Milk, divided
2 teaspoons vanilla extract
6 ounces white confectioners coating* or premium white chocolate chips
1 tablespoon peppermint extract
Green or red food coloring (optional)

Directions

In heavy saucepan, over low heat, melt chocolate chips with 1 cup sweetened condensed milk; add vanilla. Spread half the mixture into wax-paper-lined 8- or 9-inch square pan; chill 10 minutes or until firm. Hold remaining chocolate mixture at room temperature.

In heavy saucepan, over low heat, melt white confectioners coating with remaining sweetened condensed milk (mixture will be thick). Add peppermint extract and food coloring (optional).

Spread on chilled chocolate layer; chill 10 minutes longer or until firm.

Spread reserved chocolate mixture on mint layer. Chill 2 hours or until firm. Turn onto cutting board; peel off paper and cut into squares. Store leftovers covered in refrigerator.

Irish Cream Truffle Fudge

Ingredients

3 cups semisweet chocolate chips
1 cup white chocolate chips
1/4 cup butter
3 cups confectioners' sugar
1 cup Irish cream liqueur
1 1/2 cups chopped nuts

1 cup semisweet chocolate chips
1/2 cup white chocolate chips
4 tablespoons Irish cream liqueur
2 tablespoons butter

Directions

Butter a 8x8 inch pan.

In the top half of a double boiler melt the 3 cups semisweet chocolate chips, 1 cup white chocolate chips and 1/4 cup butter until soft enough to stir.

Stir in the confectioner's sugar and Irish cream until mixture is smooth. Stir in nuts. Place mixture in the prepared pan and lay a sheet of plastic wrap over top; press and smooth top down.

In the top half of a double boiler melt remaining chocolates until soft. Remove from heat and with a fork beat in the butter and Irish cream until smooth. Spread topping over cooled fudge with a knife. If a smooth top is important place plastic wrap over the top.
Refrigerate until firm, 1 to 2 hours at least. This fudge can be easily frozen.

Pudding Fudge

Ingredients

(3.5 ounce) package non-instant chocolate pudding mix
/3 cup white sugar
/2 cup brown sugar
/2 cup heavy cream
tablespoon butter

Directions

Generously butter a small pan.

Combine pudding mix, white sugar, brown sugar and cream in a large microwave-safe bowl; stir well to combine. Microwave on high until it boils, about 4 minutes. Continue to boil in microwave 3 minutes more. Stir in butter and beat until mixture begins to thicken. Spread into prepared pan and allow to cool completely before cutting into squares.

Surprise Fudge

Ingredients

8 ounces process cheese (eg. Velveeta), cubed
3/4 cup unsalted butter, cubed
1 teaspoon vanilla extract
1 cup chopped nuts
3 3/4 cups confectioners' sugar
1/2 cup baking cocoa

Directions

In a small saucepan, cook and stir the cheese and butter over medium heat until melted. Remove from the heat; stir in the vanilla and nuts. In a mixing bowl, combine the confectioners' sugar and cocoa. Add the cheese mixture and beat until combined (mixture will be stiff). Spread until a greased 9-in. square pan. Refrigerate until firm. Cut into squares. Store in refrigerator.

Easy Creamy Vanilla Fudge

Ingredients

3 3/4 cups confectioners' sugar
5 tablespoons butter
3 tablespoons milk
1 tablespoon vanilla extract
1 pinch salt

Directions

Grease a 9x5 inch pan. Set aside.

In a 3 quart saucepan, over very low heat, mix together confectioners sugar, butter, milk, vanilla, and salt until mixture is creamy.

Pour quickly into greased 9x5 inch pan. Refrigerate until firm, then cut into squares. Store in an airtight container in the refrigerator.

Fudge Truffle Cheesecake

Ingredients

Chocolate Crumb Crust
1 1/2 cups vanilla wafer crumbs
6 tablespoons confectioners' sugar
1/3 cup unsweetened cocoa powder
1/3 cup butter, melted

3 (8 ounce) packages cream cheese, softened
1 (14 ounce) can EAGLE BRANDB® Sweetened Condensed Milk
1 (12 ounce) package semisweet chocolate chips, melted
4 eggs
2 teaspoons vanilla extract
Melted semi-sweet chocolate (optional)

Directions

Preheat oven to 300 degrees F. Prepare Chocolate Crumb Crust.

Chocolate Crumb Crust: In medium bowl, combine vanilla wafer crumbs (about 45 wafers), confectioners' sugar, cocoa powder and butter. Press firmly on bottom and 1/2 inch up side of 9-inch springform pan.

In large bowl, beat cream cheese until fluffy. Gradually beat in sweetened condensed milk until smooth. Add remaining ingredients; mix well.

Pour into prepared pan.

Bake 1 hour and 5 minutes or until center is set.

Cool. Chill in refrigerator at least 4 hours.

To serve, drizzle with additional melted chocolate if desired. Store leftovers covered in refrigerator.

Jif® Peanut Butter Fudge

Ingredients

Crisco® Original No-Stick
Cooking Spray
3 cups granulated sugar
1/2 cup butter or margarine
2/3 cup PET® Evaporated Milk
1 2/3 cups Jif® Creamy Reduced
Fat Peanut Spread
1 (7 ounce) jar marshmallow
creme
1 teaspoon vanilla

Directions

Line a 13 x 9 x 2-inch pan with aluminum foil and then spray with a no-stick cooking spray.

Combine sugar, butter and milk in large saucepan, stirring constantly on medium heat, until mixture comes to a boil.

Boil 5 minutes, stirring constantly. Remove from heat.

Add peanut butter. Stir until well blended. Add marshmallow creme and vanilla. Beat until well blended.

Spread in prepared pan. Cool.

Cut into candy-sized pieces. Store in covered container.

Foolproof Chocolate Fudge

Ingredients

3 cups semisweet chocolate chips
1 (14 ounce) can sweetened
condensed milk
1/2 cup coarsely chopped walnuts
1 1/2 teaspoons vanilla extract

Directions

Line one 8 or 9 inch square pan with wax paper.

In a heavy saucepan, over low heat, melt the chocolate chips with the condensed milk. Remove from heat and stir in the chopped nuts and vanilla extract. Spread mixture evenly into the prepared pan and chill for 2 hours or until firm. Once firm, turn fudge onto cutting board, peel off waxed paper and cut into small squares.

Triple Fudge Cookies

Ingredients

(1 ounce) squares semisweet
hocolate, chopped
(1 ounce) square unsweetened
hocolate, chopped
tablespoons butter, softened
eggs
cup white sugar
/4 cup all-purpose flour
/2 teaspoon baking powder
cup semisweet chocolate chips
/4 cup chopped walnuts
teaspoon vanilla extract
/4 teaspoon salt

Directions

Preheat oven to 350 degrees F. Grease cookie sheets.

Melt the chocolate squares and butter or margarine in a double
boiler. Stir well and remove from heat.

Cream sugar and eggs in medium sized bowl until thick and
creamy. Mix in vanilla and melted chocolate.

Mix in the flour, baking powder and salt until well blended. Stir in
chocolate chips and nuts.

Drop by teaspoonfuls about 1 1/2 inches apart on cookie sheet. Bake
for 8 minutes or until tops crackle and look shiny.   Cool 3 to 5 minutes.
Remove to racks; cool completely.

Hot Fudge Ice Cream Dessert

Ingredients

1 cup miniature marshmallows
3/4 cup evaporated milk
1/2 cup semisweet chocolate chips
1/4 cup butterscotch chips
1/4 cup milk chocolate chips
10 vanilla wafers
2 pints butter pecan ice cream, softened
9 pecan halves, toasted
4 maraschino cherries

Directions

For fudge sauce, in a saucepan, combine the marshmallows, milk and chips. Cook and stir over low heat until mixture is melted and smooth. Remove from the heat and refrigerate until chilled.

Line the bottom of a 6-in. springform pan with vanilla wafers. Top with about 1 cup ice cream; press into a smooth layer. Top with a third of the fudge sauce. Freeze for 30 minutes or until set.

Repeat layers twice, freezing in between layers. Top with pecans and cherries. Cover and freeze until firm. Remove from freezer 10 -15 minutes before serving.

Remarkable Fudge

Ingredients

1 cup butter
12 ounces semisweet chocolate chips
1 (7 ounce) jar marshmallow creme
1 cup chopped walnuts
1 teaspoon vanilla extract
1 1/4 cups evaporated milk
4 cups white sugar

Directions

Line a 13x9 inch baking dish with foil and butter the foil.

In the top half of a double boiler combine the butter or margarine, evaporated milk and sugar. Cook on medium heat for 12 minutes or until it reaches a temperature of 236 degrees F (112 degrees C). Remove from heat and stir in the chocolate chips, vanilla and marshmallow creme. Stir until chocolate chips melt then mix in the chopped walnuts. Spread mixture into the prepared pan. Score into squares while still warm. Refrigerate until firm then cut along the scored lines.

Homemade Yummy Fudge

Ingredients

6 ounces cream cheese, softened
1/8 teaspoon salt
1/2 teaspoon vanilla extract
4 cups confectioners' sugar, sifted
4 (1 ounce) squares unsweetened chocolate, melted and cooled
1 cup chopped walnuts

Directions

Line an 8x8 inch dish with foil.

In a medium bowl, beat cream cheese until smooth. Beat in salt and vanilla. Beat in confectioners' sugar, a little at a time, until smooth. Stir in melted chocolate. Fold in walnuts. Spread into prepared pan. Chill 1 hour, until firm. Cut into one inch squares.

Sweetheart Fudge Cake

Ingredients

(18.25 ounce) package chocolate fudge cake mix
teaspoon vanilla extract
/4 cup currant jelly
/4 cup whipping cream
(1 ounce) squares semisweet chocolate, chopped
(16 ounce) can vanilla frosting
(8 ounce) carton frozen whipped topping, thawed
pints fresh raspberries

Directions

Grease and flour two 9-in. heart-shaped or round baking pans. Prepare cake mix according to package directions; stir in vanilla. Pour into prepared pans. Bake at 350 degrees F for 25-30 minutes or until a toothpick inserted near the center comes out clean. Cool for 15 minutes before removing from pans to wire racks.

While cakes are still warm, poke several holes in cakes with a wooden skewer to within 1/4 in. of bottom. Brush jelly over top and sides of cakes. In a small saucepan, combine cream and chocolate; cook and stir over low heat until chocolate is melted. Brush over top and sides of cakes several times, allowing mixture to absorb between brushings. Cool completely.

In a mixing bowl, beat frosting until fluffy; fold in whipped topping. Place one cake on a serving plate; spread with frosting. Top with second cake; spread remaining frosting over top and sides. Garnish with raspberries. Refrigerate for 2 hours before cutting.

Glendora's Chocolate Fudge Pudding (Cake)

Ingredients

1 cup all-purpose flour
2 teaspoons baking powder
2/3 cup white sugar
2 tablespoons unsweetened cocoa powder
1 teaspoon salt
1/2 cup milk
2 tablespoons vegetable oil
1 teaspoon vanilla extract
1/2 cup chopped walnuts (optional)
1 cup brown sugar
1/4 cup unsweetened cocoa powder
1 1/2 cups boiling water

Directions

Preheat an oven to 350 degrees F (175 degrees C). Grease a shallow 1 quart baking dish.

Whisk flour, baking powder, white sugar, 2 tablespoons cocoa powder, and salt together in a large bowl. Mix in the milk, oil, and vanilla extract. Stir in nuts. Pour batter into prepared baking dish.

Mix brown sugar and remaining 1/4 cup cocoa powder together; sprinkle over batter in baking dish. Pour the boiling water slowly over the top of the batter and topping.

Bake in the preheated oven for 40 minutes. The top of the cake will be set and the bottom will be soft. Invert hot cake onto a platter to serve.

Cookies 'n' Creme Fudge

Ingredients

3 (6 ounce) packages white
chocolate baking squares
1 (14 ounce) can EAGLE BRAND®
Sweetened Condensed Milk
1/8 teaspoon salt
3 cups coarsely crushed
chocolate creme-filled sandwich
cookies

Directions

In heavy saucepan, over low heat, melt white chocolate squares, sweetened condensed milk and salt. Remove from heat; stir in crushed cookies.

Spread evenly into wax-paper-lined 8-inch square pan. Chill 2 hours or until firm.

Turn fudge onto cutting board; peel off paper and cut into squares. Store leftovers covered in refrigerator.

Hot Fudge Sauce

Ingredients

1 (14 ounce) can sweetened condensed milk
4 (1 ounce) squares semisweet chocolate
2 tablespoons butter (no substitutes)
1 teaspoon vanilla extract

Directions

In a heavy saucepan, combine the milk, chocolate and butter. Cook and stir over medium-low heat until chocolate is melted. Remove from the heat; stir in vanilla.

Spiced Pumpkin Fudge

Ingredients

cups granulated sugar
cup packed light brown sugar
/4 cup butter or margarine
/3 cup NESTLE® CARNATION®
Evaporated Milk
/2 cup LIBBY'S® 100% Pure
Pumpkin
teaspoons pumpkin pie spice
cups NESTLE® TOLL HOUSE®
Premier White Morsels
(7 ounce) jar marshmallow
reme
cup chopped pecans
1/2 teaspoons vanilla extract

Directions

Line 13 x 9-inch baking pan with foil.

Combine sugar, brown sugar, evaporated milk, pumpkin, butter and spice in medium, heavy-duty saucepan. Bring to a full rolling boil over medium heat, stirring constantly. Boil, stirring constantly, for 10 to 12 minutes or until candy thermometer reaches 234 degrees F to 240 F (soft-ball stage).

Quickly stir in morsels, marshmallow creme, nuts and vanilla extract. Stir vigorously for 1 minute or until morsels are melted. Immediately pour into prepared pan. Let stand on wire rack for 2 hours or until completely cooled. Refrigerate tightly covered. To cut, lift from pan; remove foil. Cut into 1-inch pieces. Makes about 3 pounds.

Easy Fudge Brownies

Ingredients

2/3 cup shortening
2 tablespoons unsweetened cocoa powder
1 cup white sugar
2 eggs
1/2 cup all-purpose flour
1 teaspoon vanilla extract

Directions

Preheat oven to 350 degrees F (175 degrees C). Grease a 9-inch square baking pan.

Melt shortening and cocoa in the top of a double boiler over low heat. Stir occasionally until shortening is melted. Remove from heat. Stir in sugar, eggs and vanilla until well blended. Slowly add in flour and mix well. Spread batter evenly in pan.

Bake 18 to 20 minutes, until toothpick inserted in the center of brownies comes out clean. Let cool before cutting.

Fudge Pie

Ingredients

 recipe pastry for a 9 inch single
rust pie
 cup white sugar
/4 cup all-purpose flour
 tablespoons unsweetened
ocoa powder
/2 cup butter
 eggs
 teaspoon vanilla extract

Directions

Unfold piecrust; fit into 9 inch pie pan. Prebake crust according to package directions. Remove from oven.

Lower the oven temperature to 325 degrees F (165 degrees C).

Beat together sugar, flour, cocoa powder, butter or margarine, eggs and vanilla in a medium-size bowl. Spoon into pie shell.

Bake for 25 to 30 minutes or until set. Allow to cool to room temperature. Serve with whipped topping or a scoop of vanilla ice cream.

Ribboned Fudge Cake

Ingredients

1 (18.25 ounce) package chocolate cake mix
1 (8 ounce) package cream cheese, softened
2 tablespoons butter, softened
1 tablespoon cornstarch
1 (14 ounce) can sweetened condensed milk
1 egg
1 teaspoon vanilla extract

Directions

Preheat oven to 350 degrees F (175 degrees C). Grease and flour a 10 inch Bundt pan.

Prepare cake according to directions on package. Pour into Bundt pan.

In a medium bowl, beat together cream cheese, butter (or margarine) and cornstarch until fluffy. Gradually beat in sweetened condensed milk, egg and vanilla until smooth.

Pour cream cheese mixture evenly over cake batter.

Bake at 350 degrees F (175 degrees C) for 50 to 55 minutes. Cool for 10 minutes in the pan, then turn out onto a wire rack and cool completely. Glaze with Chocolate Glaze, or as desired.

Raspberry Truffle Fudge

Ingredients

cups semi-sweet chocolate
hips

(14 ounce) can sweetened
ondensed milk

1/2 teaspoons vanilla extract
alt to taste

/4 cup heavy cream

/4 cup raspberry flavored liqueur

cups semi-sweet chocolate
hips

Directions

Spray a 9x9 inch pan with non-stick cooking spray, and line with wax paper.

In a microwave-safe bowl, combine 3 cups chocolate chips and sweetened condensed milk. Heat in microwave until chocolate melts, stirring occasionally. Be careful not to let it scorch. Stir in the vanilla and salt. Spread into pan, and cool to room temperature.

In a microwave-safe bowl, combine cream, liqueur, and 2 cups chocolate chips. Heat in microwave until the chocolate melts; stir until smooth. Cool to lukewarm, then pour over the fudge layer. Refrigerate until both layers are completely set, about 1 hour. Cut into 1 inch pieces.

Fudge Sundae Sauce

Ingredients

2 cups semisweet chocolate chips
2 (1 ounce) squares unsweetened chocolate
1 cup heavy whipping cream
1/4 cup strong brewed coffee, cold
Dash salt
1 teaspoon vanilla extract

Directions

In a heavy saucepan, melt the chocolate with the cream, coffee and salt over low heat, stirring constantly. Remove from the heat; stir in vanilla. Cover and refrigerate. Reheat to serve over your favorite ice cream.

Easy Chocolate Fudge Cake

Ingredients

(18.25 ounce) package chocolate cake mix

/4 cup butter
cups white sugar
tablespoons unsweetened cocoa powder
cup heavy whipping cream
tablespoon vanilla extract
/4 cup chopped walnuts

Directions

Bake a box chocolate cake as directed. While hot from the oven, poke holes over entire cake with a fork. While the cake is cooking prepare the fudge sauce.

For the fudge sauce: In a saucepan, combine butter, sugar, cocoa and cream. Stir over medium heat until a full boil starts. Cook at a full boil for 2 minutes. Stir in vanilla. Pour while hot over warm cake. Sprinkle with chopped walnuts. Serve alone or with ice-cream.

Old-Fashioned Fudge

Ingredients

3 tablespoons butter
3 cups white sugar
3 tablespoons cornstarch
1 pinch salt
1 teaspoon distilled white vinegar
1 cup evaporated milk
3 (1 ounce) squares unsweetened chocolate
1 teaspoon vanilla extract

Directions

Butter an 8 or 9 inch square pan. Set aside.

In a large bowl, combine sugar, cornstarch, and salt; mix well. In a heavy saucepan, cook butter or margarine until golden brown; remove from heat. Add sugar mixture; mix well. Stir in vinegar and milk; return to heat. Bring to a boil, stirring frequently. Cover and boil 5 minutes, stirring occasionally.

Stir in chocolate. Insert a candy thermometer and cook, uncovered to soft ball stage, 238 degrees F (114 degrees C). Remove from heat; add vanilla and do not stir. Let it sit until pan is lukewarm and easy to hold.

With a sturdy wooden spoon, beat the fudge until it loses is shine.

With buttered hands, quickly press mixture into prepared pan. Let cool slightly before cutting. Keep fudge covered tightly with plastic wrap.

Fudge Brownies I

Ingredients

cup butter

(1 ounce) squares unsweetened chocolate

cups white sugar

eggs

cup all-purpose flour

teaspoon vanilla extract

/2 teaspoon salt

cups chopped walnuts

Directions

Preheat oven to 350 degrees F. Grease a 9x13 inch baking pan.

In 3-quart saucepan over very low heat, melt butter or margarine and chocolate, stirring the mixture constantly. Remove from heat, and stir the sugar into the chocolate. Allow the mixture to cool slightly. Beat in the eggs one at a time, mixing well after each, then stir in the vanilla. Combine the flour and salt; stir into the chocolate mixture. Fold in the walnuts. Spread the batter evenly into the prepared pan.

Bake in oven 30 to 35 minutes. Brownies are done when toothpick inserted into center come out clean. Cool in pan on wire rack.

Penuche Sugar Fudge

Ingredients

4 cups brown sugar
1 cup heavy cream
2 tablespoons butter
1 teaspoon vanilla
1 2/3 cups finely chopped pecans

Directions

In a medium saucepan, combine brown sugar, cream and butter. Stir until dissolved. Heat to between 234 and 240 degrees F (112 to 116 degrees C), or until a small amount of syrup dropped into cold water forms a soft ball that flattens when removed from the water and placed on a flat surface. Remove from heat and stir vigorously until mixture loses its gloss, or process in a food processor 30 seconds. Quickly stir in vanilla and nuts and spread into a 9x9 inch dish. Chill before cutting into squares.

Caramel Fudge Cheesecake

Ingredients

- 1 (10.25 ounce) package fudge brownie mix
- 1 (14 ounce) package caramels
- 1/4 cup evaporated milk
- 1 1/4 cups coarsely chopped pecans
- 2 (8 ounce) packages cream cheese, softened
- 1/2 cup sugar
- 2 eggs
- 2 (1 ounce) squares semisweet chocolate, melted
- 1 (1 ounce) squares unsweetened chocolate, melted

Directions

Prepare brownie batter according to the package directions. Spread into a greased 9-in. springform pan. Bake at 350 degrees for 20 minutes. Cool for 10 minutes on a wire rack.

Meanwhile, in a microwave-safe bowl, melt caramels with milk. Pour over brownie crust; sprinkle with pecans.

In a mixing bowl, combine the cream cheese and sugar; mix well. Add eggs, beating on low speed just until combined. Stir in melted chocolate. Pour over pecans.

Bake at 350 degrees for 35-40 minutes or until the center is almost set. Cool on a wire rack for 10 minutes. Run a knife around edge of pan to loosen; cool completely. Chill overnight.

Remove sides of pan before serving. Store leftovers in the refrigerator.

Spicy Pumpkin Fudge

Ingredients

1 cup almonds
3 cups white sugar
1 cup butter
1 (5 ounce) can evaporated milk
1/2 cup canned pumpkin
1 teaspoon pumpkin pie spice
2 cups butterscotch chips
1 (7 ounce) jar marshmallow creme
1 teaspoon vanilla extract

Directions

Butter a 9x13 inch pan and set aside.

Preheat oven to 300 degrees F (150 degrees C). Arrange almonds on a cookie sheet and place in oven to toast. Stir frequently. Do not burn. Remove from oven and set aside.

In a heavy saucepan, combine sugar, butter, milk, pumpkin, and spice; bring to a boil, stirring constantly. Continue boiling over medium heat until mixture reaches 234 degrees F (118 degrees C) on a candy thermometer, about 10 minutes.

Remove from heat. Stir in butterscotch chips. When chips are melted, add marshmallow cream, nuts, and vanilla. Mix until well blended.

Immediately pour butterscotch mixture into prepared pan. Spread evenly. Cool at room temperture. Cut into squares, and store in the refrigerator in an air-tight container.

Easy Cinnamon Fudge

Ingredients

cups confectioners' sugar
/2 cup unsweetened cocoa
owder
/2 teaspoon ground cinnamon
/2 cup butter
/4 cup milk
1/2 teaspoons vanilla extract
cup chopped walnuts (optional)

Directions

Line an 8x8 inch baking pan with aluminum foil, allowing foil to hang over the edges. Grease the foil.

In a medium bowl combine confectioners' sugar, cocoa and cinnamon.

Heat butter and milk in a medium saucepan over medium heat. When butter is melted stir in vanilla. Remove from heat and stir in sugar mixture and walnuts.

Pour into prepared pan. Refrigerate for 1 hour, or until firm.

Lift foil out of pan. Cut fudge into 2 inch squares, and then cut in half diagonally to make triangles.

Hot Fudge Pudding Cake I

Ingredients

1 1/2 cups baking mix
1/2 cup white sugar
2 tablespoons unsweetened cocoa powder
3/4 cup chopped walnuts
1/2 cup milk
1 teaspoon vanilla extract
3/4 cup packed brown sugar
1/4 cup unsweetened cocoa powder
1 1/2 cups boiling water

Directions

Preheat oven to 350 degrees F (175 degrees C).

In an ungreased 8 inch square baking pan combine the biscuit mix, white sugar, 2 tablespoons cocoa, nuts, milk, and vanilla blend well.

Combine brown sugar and 1/4 cup cocoa. Spoon evenly over top of cake mix. Do no stir. Pour the boiling water carefully over everything. Do not stir.

Bake at 350 degrees F (175 degrees C) for 35 to 40 minutes. Allow cake to cool in pan for 20 minutes before serving. Serve with whipped cream or vanilla ice cream.

Fudge Cake

Ingredients

1/2 cups white sugar
teaspoon vanilla extract
eggs
cup milk
tablespoon fresh lemon juice
/2 cup unsweetened cocoa
owder
cup hot water
1/2 cups all-purpose flour
teaspoon baking soda
teaspoon baking powder
/2 teaspoon salt
/2 cup butter

Directions

Cream butter or margarine and sugar together in a large bowl. Add vanilla, and then eggs to the mixture.

In another bowl, mix together flour, soda, baking powder, and salt. Sour the milk by adding the lemon juice or vinegar. Add flour mixture alternately with soured milk to the creamed mixture.

Mix cocoa and hot water together, and beat into batter.

Bake 30 to 35 minutes at 350 degrees F (175 degrees C). Cool, and frost with desired frosting.

Peanutty Chocolate Fudge

Ingredients

1 1/2 cups granulated sugar
2/3 cup NESTLE® CARNATION® Evaporated Milk
2 tablespoons butter or margarine
1/4 teaspoon salt
2 cups miniature marshmallows
1 (11 ounce) package NESTLE® TOLL HOUSE® Peanut Butter & Milk Chocolate Morsels
1/2 cup chopped peanuts
1 teaspoon vanilla extract

Directions

LINE 8-inch-square baking pan with foil.

COMBINE sugar, evaporated milk, butter and salt in medium, heavy-duty saucepan. Bring to a full rolling boil over medium heat, stirring constantly. Boil, stirring constantly, for 4 to 5 minutes. Remove from heat.

STIR in marshmallows, morsels, peanuts and vanilla extract. Stir vigorously for 1 minute or until marshmallows are melted. Pour into prepared baking pan; refrigerate for 2 hours or until firm. Lift from pan; remove foil. Cut into pieces.

Triple Fudge Brownies

Ingredients

(3.9 ounce) package instant hocolate pudding mix
cups milk
(18.25 ounce) package hocolate cake mix
cups semisweet chocolate chips
/3 cup confectioners' sugar for ecoration

Directions

Preheat oven to 350 degrees F (175 degrees C). Grease one 15x10 inch baking pan.

Prepare pudding mix according to package directions using the 2 cups milk. Whisk in the cake mix. Stir in the chocolate chips. Pour batter into the prepared pan.

Bake at 350 degrees F (175 degrees C) for 30 to 35 minutes or until the top springs back when lightly touched. Dust with confectioners' sugar. Serve with ice cream if desired.

Peanut Butter Cream Fudge

Ingredients

2 cups sugar
1 cup sour cream
1/8 teaspoon salt
1 cup peanut butter*
1 teaspoon vanilla extract

Directions

In a heavy saucepan, combine the sugar, sour cream and salt; bring to a boil. Cover and simmer for 5 minutes. Uncover and cook over medium heat until a candy thermometer reads 238 degrees F (soft-ball stage). Remove from the heat; stir in peanut butter and vanilla. With a wooden spoon, beat until thick and creamy, about 5 minutes. Transfer to a buttered 8-in. square dish. Cool and cut into squares. Store in the refrigerator.

Country House Fudge

Ingredients

4 1/2 cups white sugar
1 teaspoon salt
1/2 cup butter
1 (12 fluid ounce) can evaporated milk
2 cups semisweet chocolate chips
4 (4 ounce) bars German sweet chocolate
7 ounces chocolate candy bar
1 (7 ounce) jar marshmallow creme
2 teaspoons vanilla extract
2 cups chopped walnuts

Directions

Butter 2 - 9x13 inch pans. Set aside.

In a large bowl, place chocolate chips and broken up chocolate bars. Make a depression in chocolate pieces, then scoop marshmallow creme into it.

In a medium saucepan, cook sugar, salt, butter, and milk for about 8 to 10 minutes. (Start timing after boiling begins) Remove from heat, add chocolate chip mixture, vanilla, and chopped nuts. Mix RAPIDLY with large wooden spoon. Pour into buttered pans.

Deep Dish Fudge Brownies

Ingredients

3/4 cup all-purpose flour
3/4 cup cake flour
1/4 teaspoon baking powder
1/4 teaspoon salt
1 cup butter, softened
4 (1 ounce) squares unsweetened chocolate
1 3/4 cups white sugar
4 eggs
2 teaspoons vanilla extract
1 cup semisweet chocolate chips

Directions

Preheat oven to 350. Grease and flour one 9 inch square baking pan, tapping out excess flour.

Melt the butter and unsweetened chocolate in the top of a double boiler and then let cool for about 15 minutes.

Sift together both flours, baking powder and salt. Set aside. In Large bowl, whisk chocolate/butter mixture to blend. Beat in sugar, then vanilla, then eggs. Fold in dry ingredients and mix well. Stir in semisweet chocolate chips. Scrape batter into prepared pan, spreading evenly.

Bake at 350 degrees F (175 degrees C) for 30 to 35 minutes until set. Do not overbake. Cool in pan on a wire rack. Once cool cut into large squares.

Caramel Peanut Fudge

Ingredients

BOTTOM LAYER
 cup milk chocolate chips
/4 cup butterscotch chips
/4 cup creamy peanut butter

FILLING
/4 cup butter
 cup white sugar
/4 cup evaporated milk
 1/2 cups marshmallow creme
/4 cup creamy peanut butter
 teaspoon vanilla extract
 1/2 cups chopped salted
peanuts

CARAMEL
 (14 ounce) package individually
wrapped caramels, unwrapped
/4 cup heavy cream

TOP LAYER
 cup milk chocolate chips
/4 cup butterscotch chips
/4 cup creamy peanut butter

Directions

Lightly grease a 9x13 inch dish.

For the bottom layer: Combine 1 cup milk chocolate chips, 1/4 cup butterscotch chips and 1/4 cup creamy peanut butter in a small saucepan over low heat. Cook and stir until melted and smooth. Spread evenly in prepared pan. Refrigerate until set.

For the filling: In a heavy saucepan over medium-high heat, melt butter. Stir in sugar and evaporated milk. Bring to a boil, and let boil 5 minutes. Remove from heat and stir in marshmallow creme, 1/4 cup peanut butter and vanilla. Fold in peanuts. Spread over bottom layer, return to refrigerator until set.

For the caramel: Combine caramels and cream in a medium saucepan over low heat. Cook and stir until melted and smooth. Spread over filling. Chill until set.

For the top layer: In a small saucepan over low heat, combine 1 cup milk chocolate chips, 1/4 cup butterscotch chips, and 1/4 cup peanut butter. Cook and stir until melted and smooth. Spread over caramel layer. Chill 1 hour before cutting into 1 inch squares.

Chocolate Chip Cookie Dough Fudge

Ingredients

1/3 cup margarine, melted
2/3 cup light brown sugar, packed
1 pinch salt
3/4 cup all-purpose flour
1/4 cup semisweet mini chocolate chips

1 (8 ounce) package cream cheese, softened
1 (16 ounce) package confectioners' sugar
1 cup semisweet mini chocolate chips, melted
1 teaspoon vanilla extract

Directions

Line a 9x9 inch baking dish with aluminum foil, and set aside.

To make the cookie dough pieces, mix the melted margarine, brown sugar, and salt in a bowl. Stir in the flour to make a dough, and knead in 1/4 cup of chocolate chips. Form the dough into a disk about 1/2 inch to 3/4 inch thick, place it on a sheet of plastic wrap, and then shape the disk into a square with your hands.

Place the square piece of dough in the freezer for about 10 minutes, until cold and stiff, and then slice it into 1/2 inch square pieces. Refrigerate the dough pieces while you make the cream cheese fudge.

Mix together the cream cheese and confectioners' sugar in a bowl until smooth, and stir in the melted chocolate chips and vanilla extract.

Lightly fold in the cookie dough pieces, and spread the candy out into the prepared dish. Refrigerate at least 1 hour, or until firm, and remove the candy from the foil-lined dish. Cut into squares, and serve.

Cherry Blossom Fudge

Ingredients

3/4 cup evaporated milk
1 cup white sugar
1 pinch salt
1 (3 ounce) package cherry flavored gelatin
1 cup butter
2 cups semisweet chocolate chips
1 teaspoon vanilla extract
3/4 cup maraschino cherries, halved

Directions

Butter an 8x8 inch dish.

In a medium saucepan over medium heat, combine milk, sugar and salt. Bring to a boil and stir in gelatin. Boil 4 minutes. Remove from heat and stir in butter, chocolate chips, vanilla and cherries. Pour into prepared pan. Chill 2 hours before serving.

No Fail Fudge

Ingredients

4 1/2 cups white sugar
2 (5 ounce) cans evaporated milk
4 tablespoons water
1/2 cup butter
1 cup semisweet chocolate chips
1 cup white chocolate chips
14 ounces chocolate candy bar, broken into pieces
3 cups marshmallow creme
3 cups chopped walnuts

Directions

Grease a 9x13 inch cake pan. In a large Dutch oven or pan, mix together sugar, evaporated milk, water, and butter. Bring to a rolling boil and boil for 5 minutes.

Stir in semi-sweet and white chocolate chips., candy bars, marshmallow cream, and chopped walnuts. Mix well and pour into prepared cake pan. Cool and cut into small pieces.

EAGLE BRAND® Peanut Butter Fudge

Ingredients

(14 ounce) can EAGLE BRAND®
Sweetened Condensed Milk
1/2 cup Jif® Creamy Peanut
Butter
(6 ounce) packages white
chocolate squares or white baking
bars, chopped
1/4 cup chopped peanuts
teaspoon vanilla extract

Directions

In heavy saucepan, heat sweetened condensed milk and peanut butter over medium heat until just bubbly, stirring constantly. Remove from heat. Stir in white chocolate until smooth. Immediately stir in peanuts and vanilla.

Spread evenly into wax paper lined 8-or 9-inch square pan. Cool. Cover and chill 2 hours or until firm. Turn fudge onto cutting board; peel off paper. Sprinkle with additional chopped peanuts if desired. Cut into squares. Store leftovers covered in refrigerator.

Raspberry Fudge Brownies

Ingredients

1 cup white sugar
2 eggs
1/2 teaspoon vanilla extract
1/2 cup butter or margarine, melted
1/2 cup all-purpose flour
1/3 cup unsweetened cocoa powder
1/4 teaspoon baking powder
1/4 teaspoon salt
1/2 cup miniature chocolate chips
1/2 cup evaporated milk
1 egg yolk
4 (1 ounce) squares semisweet baking chocolate, chopped
6 ounces cream cheese, softened
2 tablespoons seedless raspberry jam
1 cup frozen whipped topping, thawed
2 drops red food coloring (optional)
16 chocolate curls (optional)

Directions

Preheat an oven to 350 degrees F (175 degrees C). Line an 8 inch square baking pan with aluminum foil.

In a large mixing bowl, beat the sugar, 2 whole eggs, and vanilla until combined. Mix in butter. In another bowl, combine the flour, cocoa powder, baking powder, and salt; stir into butter mixture, mixing just until incorporated. Fold in the chocolate chips. Pour the batter into the prepared pan.

Bake in preheated oven until a toothpick inserted in the center comes out with moist crumbs attached, 25 to 30 minutes. Cool pan on wire rack.

Whisk together the evaporated milk and egg yolk in a small saucepan. Heat over medium low, stirring constantly, until the mixture is very hot and thickens slightly; do not boil. Place the 4 ounces of chopped semisweet chocolate in a medium bowl, and slowly pour in the hot milk. Stir until the chocolate is melted and smooth. Pour the filling over the cooled brownies; refrigerate until firm, about 2 hours.

Beat the cream cheese with the raspberry jam in a large bowl until smooth. Fold in the whipped topping, and add the food coloring if desired. Top the cooled brownies with the frosting, using a cake comb to create a design. Cut brownies into 16 squares, then cut each square in half diagonally to form triangles. Garnish with chocolate curls if desired.

Jamoncillo de Leche (Mexican Fudge)

Ingredients

quart whole milk
3/4 cups white sugar
teaspoons vanilla extract
teaspoon baking soda
cinnamon stick
cup chopped pecans
4 pecan halves for garnish

Directions

Combine milk, sugar, vanilla, baking soda, and cinnamon stick in a large heavy saucepan. Bring to a boil over medium heat and cook, stirring continuously. After about 20 minutes remove the cinnamon stick. Place a candy thermometer in the pan and cook until the thermometer reaches soft-ball stage 240 degrees F (115 degrees C) or until you can see th bottom of the pan when you stir.

Remove the candy from the heat and add the chopped pecans. Beat the candy with a mixer for about 5 minutes. Pour the candy into a buttered 9x9-inch pan. Press pecan halves onto the top of the warm candy. Cool, then cut into pieces. Store candy in an airtight container.

Cranberry Fudge

Ingredients

1 (12 ounce) package fresh or frozen cranberries
1/2 cup light corn syrup
2 cups semisweet chocolate chips
1/2 cup confectioners' sugar
1/4 cup evaporated milk
1 teaspoon vanilla extract

Directions

Line bottom and sides of an 8x8 inch pan with plastic wrap. Set aside.

In a medium saucepan, bring cranberries and corn syrup to a boil. Boil on high for 5 to 7 minutes, stirring occasionally, until the liquid is reduced to about 3 tablespoons. Remove from heat.

Immediately add chocolate chips, stirring untill they are melted completely. Add confectioner's sugar, evaporated milk, and vanilla extract, stirring vigorously until mixture is thick and glossy. Pour into pan. Cover and chill untill firm.

Grandma's Peanut Butter Fudge

Ingredients

cups white sugar
(12 fluid ounce) can evaporated
milk
cup butter
cup crunchy peanut butter
(7 ounce) jar marshmallow
creme

Directions

Butter a 9x13 inch baking dish and set aside. Butter a 3 quart saucepan.

Place buttered saucepan over medium heat, and combine sugar, evaporated milk and 1 cup butter within. Heat to between 234 and 240 degrees F (112 to 116 degrees C), or until a small amount of syrup dropped into cold water forms a soft ball that flattens when removed from the water and placed on a flat surface.

Remove from heat and stir in peanut butter and marshmallow creme. Beat vigorously until smooth. Pour quickly into prepared baking dish. Let cool completely before cutting into squares.

Creamy Eggnog Fudge

Ingredients

2 cups white sugar
3/4 cup butter
2/3 cup eggnog
2 teaspoons ground nutmeg
1 teaspoon ground cinnamon
12 ounces white chocolate, chopped
1 (7 ounce) jar marshmallow cream
1 teaspoon vanilla extract
1/4 cup chopped walnuts

Directions

Grease a 9 inch square pan and set aside.

Combine the sugar, butter, eggnog, nutmeg, and cinnamon in a large saucepan. Bring to a boil, stirring occasionally to melt the butter. Once the mixture reaches a rolling boil, stop stirring, and clip a candy thermometer onto the pan.

Heat mixture to 235 degrees F (113 degrees C), or until a small amount of syrup dropped into cold water forms a soft ball that flattens when removed from the water and placed on a flat surface.

Remove the pan from the heat and stir in the white chocolate pieces, marshmallow cream, vanilla, and walnuts. Beat the mixture with a wooden spoon until fluffy and it starts to lose its gloss. Spoon into the prepared pan, spreading evenly. Cool completely, then cut into small squares for serving.

Fudge Sundae Pie

Ingredients

cup evaporated milk
cup semisweet chocolate chips
 cup miniature marshmallows
/4 teaspoon salt
/2 (12 ounce) package vanilla
afers
 quart vanilla ice cream, softened
/4 cup pecans

Directions

In a medium saucepan over medium heat, combine evaporated milk, chocolate chips, marshmallows and salt; stir until chocolate and marshmallows melt and mixture smoothes and thickens. Remove from heat and let cool.

Line a 9 inch pie plate with vanilla wafers. Spoon half of ice cream over wafers and spread evenly, then top with half of chocolate/marshmallow mixture. Repeat layers and top with pecans; freeze 3 to 5 hours, until firm.

Peppermint Fudge Pie

Ingredients

24 chocolate wafer cookies, crushed
1/2 cup butter
4 cups miniature marshmallows
1/2 cup milk
1 cup heavy whipping cream
1/2 cup crushed peppermint hard candies

Directions

Combine cookies and melted butter or margarine. Press into 9 inch pie plate. Bake at 350 degrees F (175 degrees C) for 10 minutes. Cool.

Put 3 cups marshmallows in a double boiler. Add milk, and cook until mixture melts and thickens. Cool in refrigerator for about 15 minutes.

In another bowl, whip the cream. Blend in the crushed candy and remaining 1 cup marshmallows. Fold whipped cream mixture into melted and cooled marshmallow mixture.

Pour into crust, and chill well before serving.

Chocolate Fudge Cookies

Ingredients

(18.25 ounce) package devil's
food cake mix
eggs
/2 cup vegetable oil
cup semi-sweet chocolate chips

Directions

Preheat oven to 350 degrees F (175 degrees C). Grease cookie sheets.

In a medium bowl, stir together the cake mix, eggs and oil until well blended. Fold in the chocolate chips. Roll the dough into walnut sized balls. Place the cookies 2 inches apart on the cookie sheet.

Bake for 8 to 10 minutes in the preheated oven. Allow cookies to cool on baking sheet for 5 minutes before removing to a wire rack to cool completely.

Mocha Fudge Cake

Ingredients

1 (18.25 ounce) package moist, dark chocolate cake mix
1 (3.9 ounce) package instant chocolate pudding mix
4 eggs
1/2 cup brewed coffee
3/4 cup coffee flavored liqueur
1/3 cup vegetable oil
1 (16 ounce) package dark chocolate frosting
3/4 cup coffee flavored liqueur

Directions

Preheat oven to 350 degrees F (175 degrees C). Grease and flour a Bundt or tube pan.

Combine cake mix, pudding mix, eggs, coffee, 3/4 cup liqueur, and oil with an electric mixer at low speed until moistened. Beat for two minutes at high speed. Pour batter into prepared pan.

Bake for 45 to 55 minutes, or until done. Cool for 30 minutes. Invert onto serving plate, and prick top with a fork.

Heat frosting in a small pan. Remove from heat, and stir in 3/4 cup liqueur. Drizzle glaze over top of cake, allowing it to soak in and drizzle over sides. Repeat until glaze is used up.

Crispy Fudge Treats

Ingredients

 cups crisp rice cereal
/4 cup confectioners' sugar
 3/4 cups semisweet chocolate
hips
/2 cup corn syrup
/3 cup butter or margarine
 teaspoons vanilla extract

Directions

Combine cereal and sugar in a large bowl; set aside. Place chocolate chips, corn syrup and butter in a 1-qt. microwave-safe dish. Microwave, uncovered, on high for about 1 minute; stir gently until smooth. Stir in vanilla. Pour over cereal mixture and mix well. Spoon into a greased 13-in. x 9-in. x 2-in. baking pan. Refrigerate for 30 minutes, then cut into squares. Store in the refrigerator.

Grandma's Fudge Cake

Ingredients

1 (18.25 ounce) package
chocolate cake mix
1 1/2 cups milk
8 tablespoons all-purpose flour
1 1/4 cups butter
5 tablespoons shortening
1 1/2 cups white sugar
1 teaspoon vanilla extract
1/4 cup unsweetened cocoa
powder
1 pinch salt
1 cup white sugar
1/4 cup milk
1/4 cup butter

Directions

Bake chocolate cake mix according to package directions for two 9 inch layers. Let cakes cool then split layers in half.

In a saucepan mix 1-1/2 cups milk with 8 tablespoons flour, cook until thick and set aside to cool.

Beat 1 1/4 cup of butter and 5 tablespoons shortening until fluffy. Add 1-1/2 cups sugar and mix well. Stir in the flour mixture. Beat until mixture stands in peaks. Stir in vanilla.

Spread this mixture between the cake layers and refrigerate for 2 hours.

In a saucepan combine cocoa, 1 cup sugar, salt, 1/4 cup milk, and 1/4 cup butter. Cook over low heat and bring to a boil. Boil mixture for one minute, do not stir. Remove from heat and add 1 teaspoon vanilla and beat until thick, this may take a few minutes. Once thick pour mixture over cooled cake and let drizzle down sides of cake and over top. Keep cake refrigerated.

Cherries and Chocolate Fudge

Ingredients

(14 ounce) can sweetened condensed milk
(12 ounce) package semisweet chocolate chips
/2 cup chopped almonds
/2 cup chopped candied cherries
 teaspoon almond extract
/4 cup pecan halves
/4 cup candied cherries, halved

Directions

Line an 8 x 8 inch square pan with aluminum foil.

In a microwave-safe bowl combine sweetened condensed milk and chocolate chips; microwave on high for 1 1/2 minutes, or until chocolate is melted. Stir until smooth. Stir in chopped almonds, chopped cherries and almond extract. Pour into prepared pan and spread evenly. Place pecan halves and cherry halves on top.

Cover and refrigerate for 2 hours, or until firm. Cut into 1 inch squares. Store, covered, in refrigerator.

Tunnel of Fudge Cake II

Ingredients

1 1/2 cups milk
1 (3.5 ounce) package non-instant chocolate pudding mix
1 cup semisweet chocolate chips
1 1/3 cups white sugar
3/4 cup butter, softened
1/2 cup shortening
1 teaspoon vanilla extract
4 eggs
2 cups all-purpose flour
1/2 cup unsweetened cocoa powder
1/2 teaspoon baking powder
1/2 teaspoon salt
1 cup milk
2 cups chopped walnuts

3/4 cup confectioners' sugar
1/4 cup unsweetened cocoa powder
6 tablespoons milk

Directions

In medium pan, combine 1 1/2 c milk and pudding mix. cook as directed on package Add chocolate chips and stir until melted. set aside.

Preheat oven to 350 degrees F (175 degrees C). Grease and flour a 10 inch Bundt pan or tube pan.

In large bowl, combine sugar, butter and shortening. Beat till light and fluffy. Add vanilla and eggs. Mix well.

Add flour, 1/2 c cocoa, baking powder, salt, and 1 cup milk to bowl Beat at low speed until moistened. Beat 3 minutes at medium speed. Stir in walnuts.

Reserve 2 cups of the batter. Pour remaining batter into greased and floured pan. Spoon filling in ring on top of batter, making sure it does not touch sides of pan. Spoon reserved batter over filling.

Bake at 350 F (175 degrees C) for 50 to 60 minutes or until cake springs back when touched lightly in center. Cool 1 hour in pan, then turn out onto a wire rack and cool completely.

In small bowl, combine confectioners sugar and 1/4 cup cocoa. Add enough milk for desired drizzling consistency. Spoon over top of cake, allowing some to run down sides.

Chocolate and Butterscotch Fudge

Ingredients

cups semi-swceet chocolate
hips

(14 ounce) can EAGLE BRAND®
Sweetened Condensed Milk

/2 cup chopped walnuts
optional)

teaspoon vanilla extract

cup butterscotch chips

Directions

In heavy saucepan, over low heat, melt chocolate chips with 1 cup sweetened condensed milk. Remove from heat; stir in nuts (optional) and vanilla. Spread evenly into wax-paper-lined 8- or 9-inch square pan.

In clean heavy saucepan, over low heat, melt butterscotch chips and remaining sweetened condensed milk. Spread evenly over chocolate layer.

Chill 3 hours or until firm. Turn fudge onto cutting board; peel off paper and cut into squares. Store leftovers covered in refrigerator.

Red and White Fudge

Ingredients

2 cups white chocolate chips
1/2 cup confectioners' sugar
1 (3 ounce) package cream cheese
1 (16 ounce) package vanilla frosting
3/4 cup chopped walnuts
2/3 cup sweetened-dried cranberries
1 teaspoon orange zest

Directions

Line a 9x9 inch pan with aluminum foil and spray lightly with non-stick coating. Melt chips in microwave, stir until smooth.

In a mixing bowl, combine confectioners' sugar, cream cheese and frosting; blend well. Stir in melted chips, walnuts, cranberries and orange peel. Stir well and spread mixture into the prepared pan. Refrigerate 1 hour or until firm. Cut into 1 inch squares before serving.

Peanut Butter Fudge Cake

Ingredients

cups all-purpose flour
cups white sugar
teaspoon baking soda
cup butter
/2 cup unsweetened cocoa
owder
cup buttermilk
eggs, beaten
teaspoon vanilla extract
1/2 cups creamy peanut butter
/2 cup butter
/4 cup unsweetened cocoa
owder
/3 cup buttermilk
cups sifted confectioners' sugar
teaspoon vanilla extract

Directions

Combine flour, white sugar, and baking soda in a large mixing bowl; set aside.

Melt 1 cup butter or margarine in a heavy saucepan; stir in 1/2 cup cocoa. Stir in buttermilk, and eggs until well blended. Cook over medium heat, stirring constantly, until mixture boils. Remove from heat. Mix into flour mixture, stirring until smooth. Stir in 1 teaspoon vanilla. Pour batter into a greased and floured 13 x 9 inch baking pan.

Bake at 350 degrees F (175 degrees C) for 20 to 25 minutes, or until an inserted wooden pick comes out clean. Cool 10 minutes on a wire rack. Carefully spread peanut butter over warm cake. Cool completely.

To Make Frosting: Combine 1/2 cup butter or margarine, 1/4 cup cocoa, and buttermilk in a small sauce pan. Bring to a boil over medium heat, stirring constantly. Pour over confectioners' sugar, stirring until smooth. Stir in 1 teaspoon vanilla. Spread chocolate frosting over peanut butter on cake. Cut into squares.

Crackle Top Fudge Sauce

Ingredients

1 cup confectioners' sugar
1/2 cup butter
1/2 cup heavy cream
3/4 cup semi-sweet chocolate chips
4 (1 ounce) squares unsweetened chocolate, chopped
1 1/2 teaspoons vanilla extract

Directions

In a saucepan over medium heat, combine the confectioners' sugar, butter and heavy cream. Cook, stirring constantly, until smooth. Do not allow the mixture to boil. Remove from heat, and stir in chocolate chips and unsweetened chocolate until melted and smooth. Allow the mixture to cool slightly before using. May be kept in a covered container for a few days at room temperature, or refrigerated for up to 1 week.

Duo-Chocolate Fudge

Ingredients

pound milk chocolate
pound semi-sweet chocolate
hips
1/2 tablespoons butter
cups marshmallow creme
cups chopped walnuts (optional)

(12 fluid ounce) can evaporated
ilk
cups white sugar

Directions

Lightly butter one 9x13 inch pan.

In a large bowl, combine the milk chocolate, semi-sweet chocolate, butter, marshmallow cream and nuts.

In a large saucepan over medium heat, combine the evaporated milk and sugar. Stir constantly and bring to a boil for 4 minutes.

Pour hot sugar mixture over chocolate mixture and stir with large spoon until well blended (do this quickly before fudge begins to harden). Once this is well blended, pour fudge into a buttered 9x13 inch baking pan. Spread out and smooth into pan.

Set aside to cool and harden, about 6 hours. Cut into squares when ready to serve.

Surprise Chocolate Fudge

Ingredients

1 (15 ounce) can pinto beans, rinsed and drained
1 cup baking cocoa
3/4 cup butter or stick margarine, melted
1 tablespoon vanilla extract
7 1/2 cups confectioners' sugar
1 cup chopped walnuts

Directions

In a microwave-safe dish, mash beans with a fork until smooth; cover and microwave for 1-1/2 minutes or until heated through. Add cocoa, butter and vanilla. (Mixture will be thick.) Slowly stir in sugar; add nuts. Press mixture into a 9-in. square pan coated with nonstick cooking spray. Cover and refrigerate until firm. Cut into 1-in. pieces.

Fudge Layer Cake

Ingredients

3/4 cups all-purpose flour
cup unsweetened cocoa powder
1/4 teaspoons baking soda
/8 teaspoon salt
/4 cup unsalted butter, softened
/3 cup white sugar
/3 cup packed brown sugar
eggs
teaspoons vanilla extract
1/2 cups buttermilk
/4 cup unsalted butter, softened
(16 ounce) package
onfectioners' sugar, sifted
(1 ounce) squares unsweetened
hocolate, melted
teaspoons vanilla extract

Directions

Sift together flour, cocoa, baking soda, and salt in a small mixing bowl.

In a separate bowl, cream 3/4 cup butter and white and brown sugars at medium speed until light and fluffy. Add eggs, one at a time, beating after each addition. Add 2 teaspoons vanilla. At low speed, begin by adding a little of the flour mixture to the butter mixture. Alternate with buttermilk until all are blended together. Start and end with flour.

Line bottoms of 2 9-inch pans with waxed paper; grease and flour. Pour batter in.

Bake in a preheated 350 degrees F (175 degrees C) oven for 25-30 minutes. Test with toothpick. Cool in pans for 10 minutes before turning onto racks to cool completely.

To Make Frosting: Cream together 3/4 cup butter and confectioners' sugar. Slowly add melted chocolate and 2 teaspoons vanilla. Beat until light and fluffy. Frost cooled cake.

Cathy's Peanut Butter Fudge

Ingredients

2 cups packed brown sugar
1 tablespoon butter
1/2 cup milk
1 teaspoon cornstarch
1 tablespoon water
1 teaspoon vanilla extract
1 cup creamy peanut butter

Directions

Grease an 8x8 inch square pan.

In a saucepan over medium heat, combine the brown sugar , butter and milk. cook until the mixture reaches the soft ball stage (234-240 degrees F, 112-115 degrees C).

Combine the cornstarch and water, add to the saucepan and mix well. Remove from heat and beat for 2 minutes. Stir in the vanilla and peanut butter until thoroughly blended. Spread batter evenly into the prepared pan. let cool, then cut into squares and enjoy!

Baked Fudge

Ingredients

cups white sugar
/2 cup all-purpose flour
/2 cup unsweetened cocoa
owder
 eggs, beaten
cup butter, melted
teaspoons vanilla extract
cup chopped pecans

Directions

Preheat oven to 300 degrees F (150 degrees C).

In large bowl, sift together sugar, flour and cocoa. Add eggs. Add melted butter, vanilla and pecans. Pour mixture into 8x12-inch baking pan.

Line a roasting pan with a damp kitchen towel. Place baking dish on towel, inside roasting pan, and place roasting pan on oven rack. Fill roasting pan with boiling water to reach halfway up the sides of the baking dish. Bake 50 to 60 minutes or until firm.

Orange Flavored Fudge

Ingredients

1 1/3 cups white sugar
1 (5 ounce) can evaporated milk
1/2 cup butter, melted
2 1/2 cups miniature marshmallows
1 cup semisweet chocolate chips
1 cup finely chopped pecans
1 teaspoon grated orange peel
2 tablespoons orange liqueur

Directions

In a 2 quart microwave safe dish combine sugar, evaporated milk and butter. Microwave on high for 8 minutes.

Stir and add marshmallows and chocolate chips; heat on high for 3 minutes, or until melted.

Stir in orange peel and liqueur. Chill for 2 hours, or until firm, and cut into squares.

Chocolate Pudding Fudge Cake

Ingredients

(18.25 ounce) package devil's
od cake mix
(3.9 ounce) package instant
hocolate pudding mix
cup sour cream
cup milk
/2 cup vegetable oil
/2 cup water
eggs
cups semisweet chocolate chips
tablespoons butter
cup semisweet chocolate chips

Directions

Preheat oven to 350 degrees F (175 degrees C). Grease and flour a 10 inch Bundt pan.

In a large bowl, combine cake mix, pudding mix, sour cream, milk, oil, water and eggs. Beat for 4 minutes, then mix in 2 cups chocolate chips.

Pour batter into prepared pan. Bake in the preheated oven for 40 to 50 minutes, or until a toothpick inserted into the center of the cake comes out clean. Cool 10 minutes in the pan, then turn out onto a wire rack and cool completely.

To make the glaze: Melt the butter and 1 cup chocolate chips in a double boiler or microwave oven. Stir until smooth and drizzle over cake.

Hot Fudge Sauce I

Ingredients

4 (1 ounce) squares unsweetened chocolate
1/2 cup butter
1/2 teaspoon salt
3 cups white sugar
1 (12 fluid ounce) can evaporated milk

Directions

Fill the lower pot of a double boiler half way and bring to a boil. Melt chocolate, butter, and salt together in upper pot. Add the sugar, 1/2 cup at a time, stirring after each addition.

Gradually add the evaporated milk, a little at a time and continue stirring until well mixed. Serve hot over ice cream. Extra sauce maybe stored in refrigerator and reheated in microwave.

Quick Fudge Icing

Ingredients

cup white sugar
tablespoons unsweetened
ocoa powder
/3 cup milk
tablespoons shortening
pinch salt
teaspoon vanilla extract

Directions

In a saucepan combine sugar, cocoa, milk, shortening, and salt. Bring mixture to a rolling boil, stirring constantly for 2 minutes.

Remove from heat and add vanilla and continue beating until frosting starts to thicken slightly. The frosting will be real creamy.

Ribbon-O-Fudge Popcorn Bars

Ingredients

2 cups semisweet chocolate chips
2 tablespoons shortening
3 tablespoons butter or margarine
4 cups miniature marshmallows
1 cup butterscotch chips
3 quarts popped popcorn

Directions

In a microwave or double boiler, melt chocolate chips and shortening. Chill for 15-20 minutes or until thickened.

Meanwhile, line a 9-in. square baking pan with foil; grease the foil and set pan aside. In a heavy saucepan over low heat, melt butter. Stir in marshmallows and butterscotch chips until melted and smooth. Place the popcorn in a large bowl; add marshmallow mixture and toss until coated. Firmly press half of the popcorn mixture into prepared pan. Spread chocolate mixture evenly over popcorn. Firmly press remaining popcorn mixture over chocolate. Chill for 30 minutes. Lift out of pan, using foil edges. Remove foil; cut into bars.

Caribbean Fudge Pie III

Ingredients

/4 cup butter, softened
/4 cup packed brown sugar
 eggs
 (1 ounce) squares semisweet
hocolate
 teaspoons instant coffee
ranules
 teaspoon rum flavored extract
/4 cup all-purpose flour
 cup chopped walnuts
/2 cup walnut halves
 (9 inch) pie shell

Directions

Preheat oven to 375 degrees F (190 degrees C). In a microwave-safe bowl, microwave chocolate until melted. Stir occasionally until chocolate is smooth.

Cream butter or margarine and sugar till fluffy. Beat in eggs, one at a time. Add melted chocolate, coffee, and rum; mix well. Stir in flour and chopped nuts. Pour filling into pie shell, and decorate with walnut halves.

Bake for 25 minutes. Remove pie from oven, and cool completely. Refrigerate 1 hour before serving.

Ingredients

1 tablespoon butter
1 (1 ounce) square unsweetened chocolate
1/3 cup boiling water
1 cup white sugar
2 tablespoons corn syrup
1/2 teaspoon vanilla extract

Directions

Melt butter and chocolate in medium saucepan. Add boiling water. Bring mixture to boil. Add sugar and corn syrup. Boil, stirring, for 5 minutes. Add vanilla and stir. Serve just warm over the chocolate roll.

Easy Peanut Butter Fudge

Ingredients

 pound confectioners' sugar
/2 cup peanut butter
/2 cup unsweetened cocoa
owder
 tablespoons milk
 teaspoons vanilla extract

Directions

Line a 8x8 inch square pan with wax paper.

Combine the confectioners' sugar, peanut butter, cocoa, milk and vanilla together and mix until smooth. Chill until firm then cut into squares.

Trail Mix White Fudge

Ingredients

1/2 cup dried cranberries
1/2 cup dried apricots, cut into
1/2-inch dice
1/2 cup roasted pistachios,
coarsely chopped
1/2 cup crystallized ginger, cut
into small pieces
2/3 cup granulated sugar
1 (5 ounce) can evaporated milk
1/4 teaspoon salt
8 ounces white chocolate chips
(or bar, cut into medium dice)
1 1/2 cups miniature
marshmallows

Directions

Like fruitcake batter, there's just enough fudge to hold the fruit and nuts together.

Spray an 8-inch square pan with cooking spray. Fit an 8-by-16-inch sheet of foil in the pan so that you can use the foil overhang as a handle to pull fudge from the pan.

Place cranberries, apricots, pistachios and ginger in a medium bowl. Then bring sugar, milk and salt to a full rolling boil in a medium heavy-bottomed saucepan over medium heat. Simmer, stirring constantly, until mixture thickens and starts to turn a pale caramel, about 5 minutes. Remove from heat, quickly stir in marshmallows, then chocolate, and stir vigorously until the marshmallows start to melt.

Pour mixture into bowl with fruit and nuts; continue to mix vigorously (hands work well once mixture has cooled to warm) until fruit and nuts are evenly distributed. Press fudge into prepared pan. Refrigerate until cool and hard, about 1 1/2 hours.

CPSIA information can be obtained
at www.ICGtesting.com
Printed in the USA
BVHW060628180521
607551BV00013B/1289